Ricky, the Saguaro & the Big Machines

**A Story by
Erin McLain**

**Illustrated by
Betsy Feinberg**

Although the author and publisher have made every effort to ensure that the information in this book was correct at press time, the author and publisher do not assume and hereby disclaim any liability to any party for any loss, damage, or disruption caused by errors or omissions, whether such errors or omissions result from negligence, accident, or any other cause.

Spanish translation by Oscar Tequida

Printed in the United States of America

First Printing December 2022

ISBN 978-1-956661-26-2 English Paperback
ISBN 978-1-956661-27-9 English Hardcover
ISBN 978-1-956661-34-7 Spanish Paperback
ISBN 978-1-956661-35-4 Spanish Hardcover

Published by:

 **Book Services**
www.BookServices.us

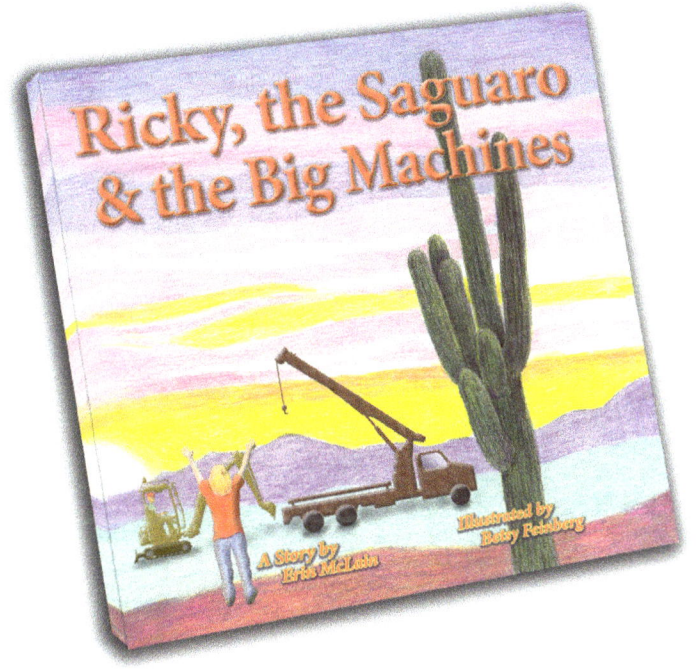

This book belongs to:

_____

Ricky's mom was excited.

Ricky's dad was excited.

Ricky was excited!

After months of searching for just the right location, they found the perfect place to build their dream house. Plus, there was plenty of room to set up a greenhouse where Ricky's father could hold horticulture workshops. Plus, their home would be right next to Saguaro National Park.

3

But when they drove out to show Ricky the property. . . .

There was a big saguaro right where the house would be!

"We aren't going to hurt the saguaro," Dad said. "We're going to move it to a safe place until the house is finished. Then we'll move it back, and we'll find the perfect place for it, just as we found the perfect place for the house." Ricky was skeptical.

"But how is that possible?" Ricky asked.

"There are companies that specialize in moving big plants," his mother explained. "They have a special storage yard where the cactus will be cared for until we're ready to welcome it back to our property. They will bundle it up so it doesn't get hurt and and lift it out of the ground with a special crane."

And that's exactly what happened. The people from the nursery came out and bundled the cactus to protect it during transit

That evening, Ricky watched as the workers loaded the saguaro onto the crane truck and drove away. They moved the saguaro at dusk to avoid the intense sun of midday.

8

They noted the orientation of the cactus to the sun. It would be placed in the storage yard in exactly the same orientation to avoid sunburn on the side of the cactus that faced north, away from the sun.

9

The next morning, Ricky woke up with a great idea! He would create a presentation on the saguaro and its unique role in the Sonoran Desert for his special project at school. He was excited about the opportunity to share everything he had learned about the saguaro with his class.

To open his presentation, Ricky created a graphic to show the height of a saguaro at different ages. He drew a picture of himself to compare the height of the cactus to the average height of an eight-year-old boy.

2"   1'   2'   3'   7'   12'   15'

5y   20y   30y   40y   50y   60-90y   100y+

13

He explained the complex relationships in the desert community. Every bird, insect, mammal, reptile, and plant has its own special place in this network. Even the soil crusts in the desert are full of tiny living creatures. They are an important part of this community, which is called an ecosystem. That's why there are signs in the parks that ask hikers to stay on the trails and not trample the biocrust, even though it might look like it is just dirt.

Palo verde trees and prickly pear cacti are important components of the Sonoran Desert ecosystem.

15

For example, when a saguaro is very little, it is protected by a nurse plant, which might be a bush, a palo verde tree, or a mesquite. Ricky showed a picture of a mesquite tree that had served as a nurse plant for the saguaro in the backyard of their rental house. The saguaro had grown right up through the mesquite!

The white-winged doves, Ricky explained, time their migration from Mexico to coincide with the flowering and ripening of fruit on the saguaro so that there is a supply of food while nesting and feeding their young. He told the class to look for white-winged doves sitting at the top of saguaros from April through September. The doves are beneficial to the cactus because they disburse the seeds in their poop.

19

Another bird that times its migration is the purple martin, a large swallow that lives in big multi-room bird houses where Ricky's family had lived in New England. But in the Sonoran desert, they nest instead in holes made by woodpeckers in saguaros or trees. Desert martins delay their migration to coincide with the arrival of the the monsoon rainy season when there are lots of insects available to feed themselves and their young.

The great-horned owl is a common bird in the desert, its nests often cradled in the arms of a large saguaro or hidden in palm trees in urban neighborhoods. Because of its height, the saguaro is a great hunting platform for the owls, who keep the rodent population under control. Ricky often heard them calling back and forth after dark. He made the whole class laugh with his imitation of a great horned owl hooting.

23

The Gila woodpecker is one of the birds responsible for the bird condos in the saguaros. It excavates a hole for its nest, uses it for one or more breeding seasons and then moves on, leaving a handy built-in birdhouse for a purple martin or a screech owl. Gila woodpeckers eat saguaro pollen and fruit, but they also locate insect meals visually as they explore the trunks and branches of mesquites and palo verde trees.

25

Ricky loved the way the male house finch's coloration matched the red of the ripe fruit of the saguaros, which provide house finches not only with food, but also with a source of liquid. They disburse the saguaro seed as they proceed with their daily activities.

One day, when Ricky was visiting Saguaro National Park, he found something strange on the trail. His father said it was coyote scat, which is a fancy way of saying poop. Coyotes are omnivores, which means they will eat anything, including saguaro fruit. To Ricky, the scat looked like a pile of saguaro seeds glued together. Coyotes also help with seed dispersal.

Ricky had an eagle eye for spotting critters, even those that were well camouflaged. One day he found a strange insect on the ground. He thought it was dead, but when he poked it with a stick, it startled him by making a loud, buzzing sound. It was a kind of cicada called a cactus dodger. His father thought the insect probably got its name because it was often found on cacti and was very good at the seemingly impossible task of dodging around the spines without getting impaled.

Ricky got a laugh out of his class when he imitated the loud buzz of the cicada.

One of Ricky's favorites was the chain-fruit cholla, the very cactus that the boy next door in New England had said would jump out and stick you. It was called chain-fruit cholla because new fruits were added at the ends of the old fruit, forming long chains.

Some people called it a jumping cholla because the spiny segments break off at the slightest touch, sticking to clothes or shoes. Because the fruit does not always produce seeds, the cholla relies mainly on fallen stem joints to create new plants.

Ricky loved the beautiful, unusual flowers. And he learned that the spineless, juicy fruits were eaten by bighorn sheep, deer, and cattle for both food and water, especially in times of drought.

It was a special treat to see a black-tailed jackrabbit when Ricky went on desert walks with his parents. The rabbit was always gone almost before Ricky could blink. That's because the placement of their eyes high on the sides of their relatively flat heads gives them almost 360° vision. They see you a split second before you see them.

Jackrabbits are herbivores, eating seeds, twigs, and cactus, but they are also an important source of food for coyotes, hawks, bobcats, and even humans.

Technically, jackrabbits are not rabbits at all, but hares. Unlike true rabbits, jackrabbit babies are born with fur and with their eyes open.

35

Harris's antelope squirrel is a ground squirrel that looks a bit like a chipmunk. It has a long white stripe on its side, and you might see it climbing through a cactus eating the seeds and fruit. It can tolerate temperatures up to 107° Fahrenheit by heat dumping, sometimes called splooting. It lies down flat, spreading its legs out and curling its tail to shade its back. It helps disburse cactus seeds. Ricky got another laugh when he suggested that his classmates try splooting when they got too hot.

Most of all, Ricky liked to talk about the saguaro. When the plant is blossoming, its pollen provides food for all sorts of insects and birds. There are over a thousand kinds of bees in the Sonoran Desert, many of them solitary bees, rather than bees that form colonies. Bees like digger bees, as well as pollinating flies and other insects, fly from plant to plant and help the saguaro set fruit.

Saguaro fruit is bright red and highly nutritious. However, it can only be harvested on private land. Only members of the Tohono O'odham Nation may harvest fruit on the reservation or in Saguaro National Park in the manner they have done for centuries. The Tohono O'odham use traditional long harvesting tools to access the fruit.

Even on your own land, you may find it difficult or impossible to get to ripe fruit before the white-winged doves. Besides, the fruit is at a height inaccessible to most people.

41

Ricky featured the stunningly beautiful two-tailed swallowtail butterfly as the grand finale of his presentation because it is the official Arizona state insect.

The adult butterfly, one of the largest north of the Mexican border, is an omnivore, feeding on milkweed, thistle flowers, and almost anything else it can find. The caterpillar's food preferences are a bit different. In southern Arizona, its food plants include Arizona rosewood and Arizona sycamore.

Ricky's presentation was so interesting that his teacher asked if he would be willing to repeat it at the public library! Wow! Of course he would.

The day came to bring the saguaro home. When it was removed for storage, a mini-excavator had reserved a pile of dirt from the original site. The workers now had dug a hole in the new location. The hole had nearly vertical sides and was almost as deep as Ricky was tall.

The crane truck lowered the cactus into the hole, and filled it with soil from the original site. Some of the microscopic creatures in the biocrust had survived and would now create an environment that was compatible with the saguaro's needs.

Ricky's dad had carefully studied the drainage in the new location to be sure it matched the original site. The workers also created a tapered mound all the way around the saguaro to divert the rainwater. The saguaro would now be on a dry regimen for six months, by which time the mound would have eroded away and the saguaro would be stable.

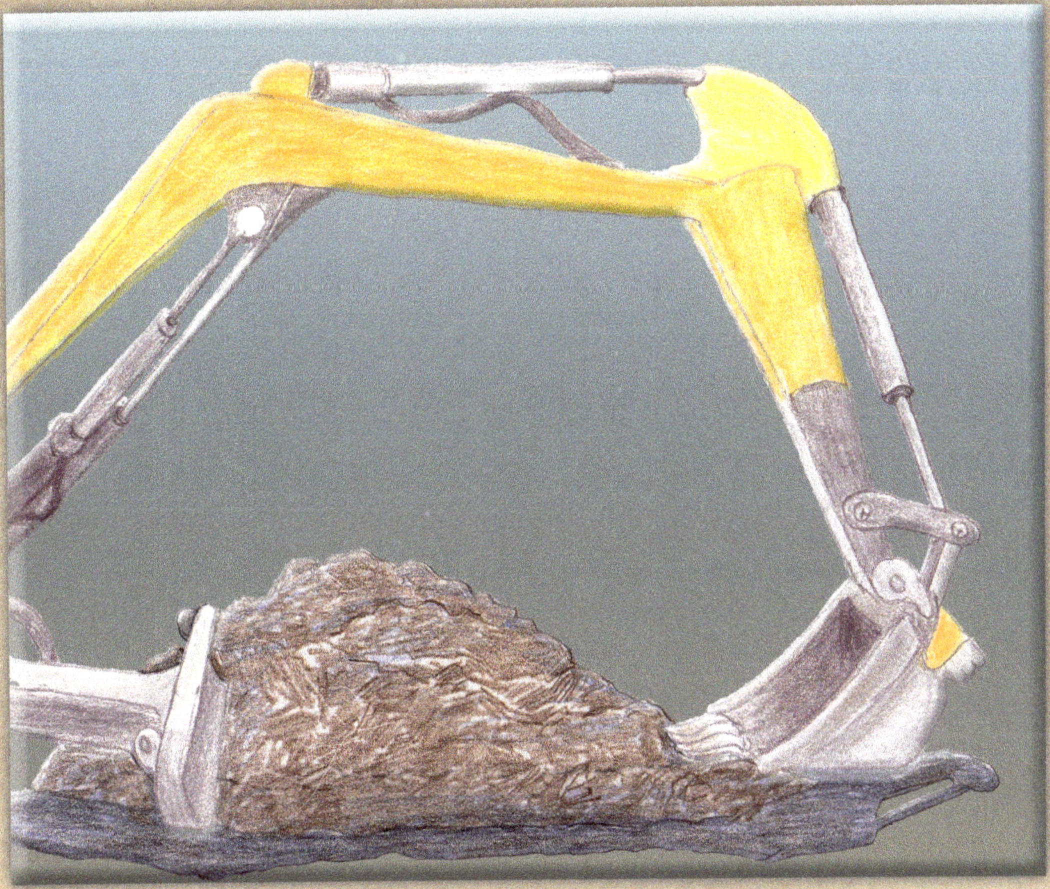

Ricky stood looking at the saguaro in front of the house for such a long time that his mom asked him if something was wrong. "No," Ricky replied. "I'm just excited because I realized what I want to do when I grow up. I want to be a horticulturist and a caretaker of the desert."

About the Author

Erin Mary McLain graduated from the University of Arizona, she moved to a rural community on the edge of Arizona's Fort Apache Reservation to fulfill her dream of community service through helping the less fortunate.

She only got to practice 21 months before her life was taken from her by a medical error after a tonsillectomy. Erin received many plaques for academic achievement. When she died, it was found that most of the boxes remained unopened. She hadn't cared about awards. Her only goal had been to become the best pediatrician she could possibly be.

About the Illustrator

Betsy Hoyt Feinberg is a writer, artist, naturalist, and illustrator who lives in the Sonora Desert, where she communes with jackrabbits, lizards, and other desert creatures, when she's not drawing animals at Tucson's Reid Park Zoo.

Erin Mary McLain, MD, FAAP Educational Foundation

Royalties from sales of this book go to the *Erin Mary McLain, MD, FAAP Educational Foundation,* whose purpose is the prevention of unnecessary deaths related to minor and major surgery and other medical procedures, as well as to fund doctors in pediatric residency who wish to establish a practice in a rural area.

"If we have healthy children, we have healthy adults."
Erin Mary McLain